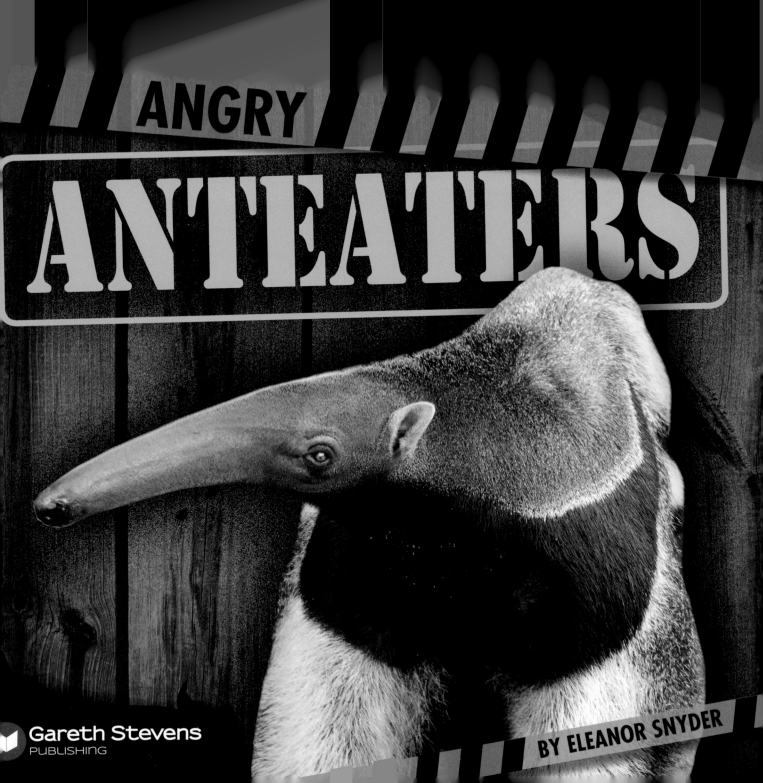

ANGRY

ANTEATERS

BY ELEANOR SNYDER

Gareth Stevens
PUBLISHING

Please visit our website, www.garethstevens.com. For a free color catalog of all our high-quality books, call toll free 1-800-542-2595 or fax 1-877-542-2596.

Library of Congress Cataloging-in-Publication Data

Names: Snyder, Eleanor, author.
Title: Angry anteaters / Eleanor Snyder.
Description: New York : Gareth Stevens Publishing, [2017] | Series: Cutest animals...that could kill you! | Includes bibliographical references and index.
Identifiers: LCCN 2016000743 | ISBN 9781482449167 (pbk.) | ISBN 9781482449105 (library bound) | ISBN 9781482448986 (6 pack)
Subjects: LCSH: Myrmecophaga–Juvenile literature. | CYAC: Anteaters.
Classification: LCC QL737.E24 S69 2017 | DDC 599.3/14–dc23
LC record available at http://lccn.loc.gov/2016000743

First Edition

Published in 2017 by
Gareth Stevens Publishing
111 East 14th Street, Suite 349
New York, NY 10003

Copyright © 2017 Gareth Stevens Publishing

Designer: Sarah Liddell
Editor: Therese Shea

Photo credits: Cover, pp. 1, 9 kungverylucky/Shutterstock.com; wood texture used throughout Imageman/Shutterstock.com; slash texture used throughout d1sk/Shutterstock.com; p. 5 (map) AridOcean/Shutterstock.com; p. 5 (main) Lenka Kozuchova/Shutterstock.com; p. 7 Luciano Queiroz/Shutterstock.com; p. 10 schankz/Shutterstock.com; p. 11 esdeem/Shutterstock.com; p. 13 belizar/Shutterstock.com; p. 14 Eric Isselee/Shutterstock.com; p. 15 Berndt Fischer/Photographer's Choice/Getty Images; p. 17 Berndt Fischer/Oxford Scientific/Getty Images; p. 19 Morales/age fotostock/Getty Images; p. 21 Wayne Lynch/All Canada Photos/Getty Images.

Printed in the United States of America

CPSIA compliance information: Batch #CS16GS: For further information contact Gareth Stevens, New York, New York at 1-800-542-2595.

CONTENTS

Words in the glossary appear in **bold** type the first time they are used in the text.

SO CUTE... AND DEADLY!

Have you ever seen an anteater? Its long **snout**, small eyes, and hairy body make it look pretty cute—and a bit funny. These **mammals** only eat bugs, mostly ants and termites. So you might think there's not much to be afraid of.

But the largest species, or kind, of anteater—the giant anteater—can be **fierce**. Even animals much larger than bugs should keep away, including people! What makes these creatures so cute but deadly? Read on to find out!

THE DANGEROUS DETAILS

There are four species of anteaters. They're found from southern Mexico to northern Argentina.

Tasha Tudor's

Bedtime
Book

For Murray Rhein,
with respectful admiration

1980 Printing
Copyright ©1977 by Platt & Munk, Publishers.
All rights reserved.
Printed in the United States of America.
Published simultaneously in Canada.
ISBN: 0-448-47217-1 (Trade Edition)
ISBN: 0-448-13038-6 (Library Edition)
Library of Congress Catalog Card Number: 77-85353

Tasha Tudor's

Bedtime
Book

Edited by Kate Klimo

Platt & Munk, Publishers/New York

A Division of Grosset & Dunlap

Goldilocks and the Three Bears

nce upon a time, three bears lived together in a house in the woods. One was a great big bear, one was a middle-sized bear, and one was a wee small bear.

One morning, they sat down to a breakfast of porridge. There was a big bowl for the great big bear, a middle-sized bowl for the middle-sized bear, and a wee bowl for the wee small bear. But the porridge was too hot to eat, so they went for a walk in the woods while it cooled.

While they were gone, a little girl named Goldilocks came by on her way through the woods. She looked in the window and saw that no one was home. Then she opened the door and walked right in.

When Goldilocks saw the porridge on the table, she helped herself. The porridge in the big bowl was too hot. The porridge in the middle-sized bowl was too cold. But the porridge in the wee bowl was just right, and she ate up every last bit of it.

Then Goldilocks sat down in a chair. The chair belonging to the great big bear was too hard. The chair belonging to the middle-sized bear was too soft. The chair belonging to the wee small bear felt just right. But as soon as Goldilocks had settled down and made herself comfortable, the bottom split and she fell to the floor.

Having broken the chair, Goldilocks went in search of a comfortable bed. The great big bed of the great big bear was too hard. The middle-sized bed of the middle-sized bear was too soft. The wee bed of the wee small bear was just right, so she climbed under the covers

and fell asleep.

The bears soon returned from their walk. They knew right away that something was wrong.

"Somebody has been eating my porridge!" said the great big bear in a great booming voice.

"Somebody has been eating my porridge," said the middle-sized bear in a middle-sized voice.

"Somebody has been eating my porridge, and it's all eaten up!" cried wee small bear in a wee squeaky voice.

So the bears set out to conduct a thorough search of the house. First they came upon the chairs.

"Somebody has been sitting in my chair!" said great big bear in a great booming voice.

"Somebody has been sitting in my chair," said middle-sized bear in a middle-sized voice.

"Somebody has been sitting in my chair, and it's broken!" cried wee small bear in a wee squeaky voice.

Then the bears went into the bedroom.

"Somebody has been lying in my bed," said great big bear in a great booming voice.

"Somebody has been lying in my bed," said middle-sized bear in a middle-sized voice.

"Somebody has been lying in my bed!" cried wee small bear in a wee squeaky voice. "And she is still here!"

At the sound of wee small bear's wee squeaky voice, Goldilocks awoke to the sight of the three bears. So startled was she that she jumped from the bed and out the nearest window. She was never again seen by the three bears—who certainly did not miss her.

The Frog Prince

Long ago, when wishes really came true, there lived a king and his beautiful daughter. She was so beautiful that the sun gave her a golden ball as a gift.

Every day when the sun was hot and high in the sky, she would sit on the cool stones of the palace well, tossing her golden ball high in the air and catching it.

One day, she accidentally tossed her golden ball into the well. She cried and cried.

"Tell me why you are crying, princess."

The princess looked up. Through her tears she saw that a frog had spoken these words.

"I am crying because my golden ball has fallen into the well, and I know I shall never get it back."

"Is that all?" said the frog. "I'll be glad to fetch it for you. But what will you give me if I do?"

"Oh dear, sweet, helpful frog," said the princess. "Anything in the world you wish for will be yours."

"All that I wish," said the frog, "is that you make me your best friend. Let me sit beside you at table, eat from your plate, and drink from your cup. Let me sleep on your pillow at night, and, princess, I will dive into that well and fetch your golden ball."

No sooner had the princess promised to grant his wish than the frog dived into the well and returned with her ball. Without so much as a word of thanks, the princess picked up the ball and skipped home to the palace. "Wait! Wait for me!" croaked the frog. But the princess did not even hear.

The next evening, the princess and the king were eating dinner when they heard a splashing and a plopping on the front step. The princess ran to the door. There, squatting on the doorstep, was the frog. She slammed the door and ran back to her place at the table.

"Whatever is the matter, daughter?" asked the king.

"It's nothing, Father, but an old green frog."

"And what does such a creature want with us?" asked the king.

"I promised the frog that if he fetched my ball from the well, I would be his best friend. But, oh, Father, I never dreamed he would leave the well."

"A promise is a promise," said the king sternly. "Now go and let in your friend."

With great reluctance, the princess opened the door. The frog followed her to her chair. "Lift me up beside you," he croaked. She shuddered but remembered her promise and placed him on the chair beside her. Then he asked to be set on the table, where he might reach her plate and cup. And when it was time for bed, he asked to sleep on the pillow by her head. There, to the princess's disgust, he stayed until just before dawn.

The next night, the frog came back, sat at the table, ate from the princess's plate, drank from her cup, and slept on the pillow by her head.

"Ugh," said the princess on the third night. "However shall I get a wink of sleep with that horrid beast on my pillow?" And she cried herself to sleep.

The next morning, the frog slid off her pillow and onto the floor. But as soon as his feet touched the floor, he was no longer a frog. He had become a handsome young prince.

"You see," he said to the surprised princess, "a wicked magician put a spell on me. Only your staying with me three nights in a row could break the spell."

Then they really did become best friends. And when they grew up, they married and lived happily together for many years.

The Three

nce there was a wood-
cutter who made a
good living at his
trade. He and his wife
had a cozy cottage,
warm clothing, and all the food they
could eat. Still, they were always wishing
for more.

One day when the woodcutter was at
work, a wood nymph appeared from
within a tree he was just about to cut.
She was as wispy and delicate as the tree
itself. "Please, woodcutter," she implored,
"spare this tree, for it is my only home,
and without it I should die." So startled
was the woodcutter that he readily
obliged.

"You shall be rewarded," said the wood
nymph. "I shall grant you three wishes.
One is for you, one is for your wife, and
the third is for you both. Tomorrow evening, I shall come to you so that you may
tell me what your third wish will be."

The woodcutter ran home to tell his
wife the good news. They joined hands
and danced with joy. Imagine having three
whole wishes come true! They talked ex-
citedly through dinner and well into the
night about all the things they might wish
for: castles with rooms of gold, acres of
land, and hundreds of suits of clothes.
Finally, unable to settle upon their wishes,
they decided to go to bed. Perhaps in the
morning they would be able to make up
their minds.

In the morning, the woodcutter and
his wife awoke to discover they were
without breakfast. The wife had been so
busy considering wishes the night before,

Wishes

that she had completely forgotten to prepare a breakfast pudding.

"Foolish woman," scolded the woodcutter. "With all your talk of castles and gold, you forgot to put up our breakfast. I'm as hungry as a bear. How I wish there were a tasty pudding here right now."

No sooner had he said these words than a plum pudding appeared on the table before the couple's startled eyes. "Clumsy fool!" cried the wife. "See how stupidly you have used your wish. You deserve to have that pudding stuck to your nose. I wish it were."

With these words, the pudding flew from the table and stuck fast to the woodcutter's nose. Though she tried with all her might, the foolish wife could not pry the pudding loose.

"Now we shall have to use that third wish to wish it off my nose," shouted the woodcutter from behind the pudding. But his wife would not agree to use their last wish in that manner.

While flies buzzed round the pudding bowl, heated words flew back and forth. By evening, however, when the wood nymph came to grant the couple's last wish, they had agreed to use the wish to unstick the pudding bowl from the woodcutter's nose.

And so the final wish was made. The plum pudding and the woodcutter at last were separated. The pudding was eaten with great gusto and proper thanks. From that day forth, the couple appreciated the good things they had had all along—and they never again wished for more.

Snow White and the Seven Dwarfs

Once upon a time, a beautiful baby girl was born to a king and queen. She had skin as white as snow, lips as red as blood, and hair as black as ebony. She was called Snow White.

As soon as Snow White was born, her mother died. A year later, the king married a second time. His new wife was beautiful, but she was jealous of anyone more beautiful than she. She had a magic mirror of which she daily asked:

"Mirror, mirror, on the wall,
Who is the fairest of us all?"

The mirror always answered:

"Thou art fairest in the land."

The years passed, and with each passing year Snow White grew more beautiful. Finally, there came a day when the queen was told by the mirror:

"Queen, thou art fair, 'tis true,
But Snow White is fairer far than you."

Upon hearing this, the queen ordered a huntsman to take Snow White into the woods and kill her. The huntsman could not kill Snow White. Instead, he left her in the woods and returned to the queen, claiming to have killed her. The queen was satisfied.

Meanwhile, Snow White wandered in the dark wood until she came upon a cottage. No one was inside, but there were seven little chairs around a table set for seven, and seven little beds. Snow White chose the largest bed and went to sleep.

In the morning, Snow White awoke to find seven dwarfs crowded round the bed, staring at her in awe, for never before had they seen such beauty. When she told them of her plight, they were only too happy to let her stay with them.

Each day the seven dwarfs marched off to the mountains to mine for gold and gems. Snow White stayed behind and kept house.

Back at the castle, the queen was not at all happy. One morning she went to her mirror to ask who was fairest, and the mirror told her that Snow White, who lived in the woods with seven little men, was fairest in the land.

The queen disguised herself as a peddler and went to the cottage of the seven dwarfs. "Would you care to buy this splendid belt?" she asked Snow White. "Let me tie it about you." Whereupon she tied the belt so tightly that Snow White fell to the floor in a swoon.

The seven dwarfs returned from the hills just in time to loosen the belt and save Snow White. But they did not catch the queen, who had long since left.

When the wicked queen reached home, the mirror reported to her that Snow White was still fairest. More jealous than ever, she made a poisoned apple.

The next day, again disguised as a peddler, the queen sold the apple to Snow White. With one bite of the luscious red apple, Snow White fell dead.

When the dwarfs came home that evening, they tried in vain to bring Snow White back to life. After all their efforts had failed, they built a lovely glass coffin so that all who passed might look upon the beautiful maiden.

One day, a prince came riding through the forest and chanced to see the coffin. He fell deeply in love with Snow White and begged the dwarfs to let him take the coffin. The dwarfs consented, for they could see that the prince's heart would break if they refused his request.

As they lifted the coffin, the morsel of poisoned apple fell from Snow White's lips and, to everyone's great joy and surprise, she began to breathe again. That very day, the prince and Snow White were married. They lived in happiness for the rest of their lives.

Shingebiss

O n the shores of the Great Lake, Shingebiss, the wild duck, made his home. During the summer, he sought his food in the shallow water along the shore. Dipping his big bill into the soft mud, he scooped up little shellfish and tadpoles and other things a wild duck likes to eat.

When the summer had passed, the mud became hard with frost. But Shingebiss didn't mind. "How fortunate it is that I have a comfortable lodge with a good fire," he said to himself. "Fortunate, too, that I have such a strong bill."

Shingebiss left his lodge and went down to the lake. The water was frozen from shore to shore. He walked along until he saw a bunch of frozen rushes standing up above the ice. Then, with his strong bill, he pulled them up and made a hole in the ice. There were fish swimming under the ice. Soon Shingebiss had a nice long string of them to take home for supper.

Far up in the Arctic lived the North Wind. He was a quarrelsome creature. He liked to come blowing down over the earth, frightening the animals and birds. "I think I'll go down and blow over the Great Lake," he growled to himself one cold day.

As he blew, the deer and rabbits huddled in their homes. The squirrels rolled themselves up in hollow trees and went to sleep.

But Shingebiss went about his usual business. He walked down to the hole he had made in the ice the day before. It was frozen over. With his strong bill, Shingebiss opened it up again. Then he fished for his supper.

"Whoo! Whoo! Whoo!" howled the North Wind, swirling around the duck. But Shingebiss paid him no attention. He had a coat of feathers and down that kept him warm and comfortable. He feared no wind.

When he had caught as many fish as he wanted, Shingebiss went back to his lodge, singing a song his mother had

taught him when he was a tiny duckling.

> "Oh, North Wind, why frighten
> others?
> In nature's family, all are
> brothers."

The North Wind heard this and laughed scornfully, "When I blow, all living creatures must hide!"

> "Puff and blow and wheeze and
> hiss,
> You can't frighten Shingebiss!"

sang the duck, as he cooked his supper.

"We'll see whether you are as brave as you say," said the North Wind. Then he swept away over the lake and, with his cold breath, froze the ice thick over the hole where Shingebiss fished.

Next morning, Shingebiss went to fish and found the ice too thick to break. He walked along the shore until he saw a clear place with frozen rushes standing up. With his strong bill, he pulled out the rushes and fished through the hole he had made.

When Shingebiss was back at the lodge cooking supper, the North Wind appeared. "Whoo! Whoo! Whoo!" he shouted. "I'll blow your lodge down."

But Shingebiss had built his lodge so well that it did not bend or sway when the wind blew. Gaily, he sang:

> "Bring your frost and ice and
> snow;
> I'm still free to come and go."

Then the North Wind became so angry that he lifted the window flap and whirled into the lodge. "I'll blow your fire out!" he roared. But, as he puffed, the fire only burned brighter and brighter.

"Whew!" exclaimed the North Wind, who was not used to staying in a warm room. He felt drops of water running down his face. "I'm melting!" he cried, and, lifting the flap, he rushed from the lodge.

Shingebiss sang after him:

> "You can never frighten me.
> One who doesn't fear is free!"

And the North Wind troubled Shingebiss no more.

The Sorcerer's Apprentice

A man who needed help in his workshop came upon a lad who seemed in need of a job.

"You look hungry, son. It so happens that I need an apprentice in my workshop. Can you read and write?"

"Yes, sir, indeed I can!" said the lad, who had set out to seek his fortune that very morning.

"Too bad, then, for I require an apprentice who cannot read and write."

"I beg your pardon, sir," said the lad hastily. "I really cannot read and write. I said I could only because I thought it would help me get the job."

"Excellent," said the man. "You've got the job. Come along to my workshop, and I'll set you to work."

Now, the lad knew perfectly well how to read and write, and he was suspicious of any man who had no use for such valuable skills. His suspicions deepened when he saw the workshop. It was as dark and musty as a cave. A giant copper cauldron bubbled on the hearth. The walls, dusty and cobwebby, held hundreds of books, great glass beakers, oddly shaped jars, and all sorts of queer scales and measuring devices. "Why, this man is a sorcerer!" said the lad to himself. "If I keep my eyes open, I might learn something useful."

Every day the lad did his chores. He stirred the foul-smelling brew that simmered in the cauldron. He ground up all manner of herbs. He fetched wood and kept the fire blazing in the hearth.

One night, when he was sure the sorcerer was asleep, the lad crept from his bed and carefully drew down a book from one of the shelves. Each page was covered with ancient spidery writing, mystic symbols, formulas, spells, and recipes for potions. Unable to put down the book, he read until dawn. Then, his head swimming with incantations, he crept back to bed.

The next night, the lad studied two more books, this time memorizing the formulas. Night after night, he read and studied. The more he learned, the more obvious it became to him that his employer was a wicked sorcerer.

Each day while the sorcerer was out—doing evil, no doubt—the lad practiced casting spells. He turned a cat into a mouse, then back into a cat. He turned a broom into a cello and back again.

One day, the sorcerer came in early and caught him practicing. "Lying wretch!" he cried. "So you can read and write! You've stolen my secrets!" With that, he moved to toss the lad into the boiling cauldron. The quick-witted apprentice immediately cast a spell and changed the sorcerer into a bird. But, as he flew out the door into the forest, the sorcerer uttered a stronger incantation and changed into a larger, faster bird.

Wings flapping, the sorcerer flew after his apprentice. Quick as a wink, the lad changed into a fish. Just as quickly, the sorcerer became a bigger fish. Then the boy became a gigantic fish.

In order to escape, the sorcerer was forced to cast the most powerful spell at his command. Turning himself into a kernel of corn, he rolled into a tiny crack between two stones, out of the lad's reach. Instantly, the apprentice turned himself into a rooster. With his sharp beak, he dug out the tiny kernel and gobbled it up, putting an end to the wicked sorcerer.

The apprentice then became a full-fledged sorcerer. He took over the workshop, and from that day on used all his skills to make only good magic.

The Billy Goats Gruff

There once upon a time lived three billy goats. They were called the Billy Goats Gruff. The biggest billy goat was Big Billy Goat Gruff. The middle-sized billy goat was Middle-sized Billy Goat Gruff. The littlest billy goat was Little Billy Goat Gruff.

The three Billy Goats Gruff lived in a valley. They liked to eat the fresh green grass there. They ate the grass all day long. They ate and ate until, at last, they had eaten all the fresh green grass.

"What shall we do?" asked Little Billy Goat Gruff. "There is no more grass for us to eat here. Where can we find more?"

Big Billy Goat Gruff said, "In the morning, we will go to the hills on the other side of the stream. There we will find fresh green grass. But remember, to cross the stream, we must go over a bridge. Under the bridge lives a big ugly troll who likes to eat billy goats. And he does not like anyone to go over his bridge. We must be very careful."

Early next morning, Little Billy Goat Gruff awoke and said, "I am hungry. I will go across the bridge to the hills, all by myself, and eat the grass there. I will cross the bridge very quietly, so that the big ugly troll will not hear me."

Little Billy Goat Gruff started off, and soon he came to a bridge. *Trip-trap, trip-trap,* onto the bridge he went.

"Who is walking over my bridge?" asked the big ugly troll.

"It is I," said Little Billy Goat Gruff. "I am going to the hills to eat grass."

"Oh, no, you are not!" shouted the troll. "I am coming to eat you."

"Please, Mr. Troll, don't eat me," said Little Billy Goat Gruff. "Wait for Middle-sized Billy Goat Gruff. He is bigger than I am." So the big ugly troll let the little goat go *trip-trap* across the bridge.

Soon Middle-sized Billy Goat Gruff woke up and ran to the bridge. *Trip-trap,*

trip-trap, onto the bridge he went.

"Who is walking on my bridge?" shouted the troll.

"I am Middle-sized Billy Goat Gruff. I am going to the hills on the other side of the bridge to eat grass."

The big ugly troll said, "Oh, no, you are not going to cross the bridge. I am coming to eat you."

"Oh, please don't eat me," said Middle-sized Billy Goat Gruff. "Wait for Big Billy Goat Gruff. He is bigger than I am."

"Very well," said the troll. He let the middle-sized goat cross the bridge.

Then Middle-sized Billy Goat Gruff ran off to the hills and joined Little Billy Goat Gruff. "We got away from the troll," they said, "and Big Billy Goat Gruff will get away from him, too."

Soon Big Billy Goat Gruff awoke. He did not see the other two Billy Goats Gruff. "They have gone to the hills to eat grass," he said. "I will go there, too."

Soon he came to the bridge. *Tramp,*

tramp, tramp, tramp, went Big Billy Goat Gruff onto the bridge.

The big ugly troll was waiting for Big Billy Goat Gruff. When he heard *tramp, tramp* on the bridge, he knew it was Big Billy Goat Gruff.

"Who is walking on my bridge?" said the troll.

"It is I, Big Billy Goat Gruff. I am going across your bridge. I am going to the hills to eat grass."

"Oh, no, you are not!" said the big ugly troll. "I am coming to eat you."

"Come on up," said Big Billy Goat Gruff. "I am not afraid of you!"

Up climbed the troll from under the bridge. Big Billy Goat Gruff put his head down and ran at the troll. *Bump!* went Big Billy Goat Gruff. *Splash!* went the troll, into the water.

Then Big Billy Goat Gruff joined the other two Billy Goats Gruff in the hills. There they ate grass and grew fat, and lived happily ever after.

Mother Hulda

There once was a widow who had two daughters. One was beautiful and industrious, the other ugly and lazy. The widow favored the lazy one, for she was her natural daughter, while the industrious one was her stepdaughter. And, oh, how she worked her stepdaughter! Every day, the poor girl had to sit by the well and spin until her fingers bled.

One day, the stepdaughter stained the shuttle with her blood. She dipped it in the well to rinse it clean and accidentally let it fall in. Fearing the wrath of the widow, she dived into the well after the shuttle. Immediately, she blacked out.

When she came to, the girl found herself in a lovely meadow. She walked across the meadow until she came to a baker's oven. It was filled with bread crying, "Take us out! Take us out! We're done!" The girl took the baker's shovel and removed the golden loaves.

Next, she came to an apple orchard where the apples cried, "Shake us! Shake us! We're ripe!" The girl shook each tree and heaped the fallen apples into piles.

Finally, she came upon a cottage. Out of the cottage window peeped an old lady with great big teeth. "I am Mother Hulda, child," said the woman. "Stay here and keep house for me, and you shall be rewarded. But you must make my bed, and shake it till the feathers fly. For only then will there be snow on earth."

Mother Hulda seemed kind, so the girl agreed to stay and keep house for her. Every day, she shook the bed till the feathers flew. And every day, she was courteous and cheerful. But as the days passed, she grew homesick. "I know it's not a pleasant place, but I do miss my home," she told Mother Hulda.

Mother Hulda was pleased to hear this and offered to send the girl home that very day. Handing her the shuttle, Mother Hulda led her to a great door. The girl stepped through the door and fell to earth in a shower of pure gold. As she crossed the yard to her home, the rooster cried:

> "Cock-a-doodle doo!
> Your golden girl's come home to you!"

The widow heard her stepdaughter's story. Then, greedy for more gold, she sent her lazy daughter to the well. The lazy daughter thrust her hand into a brier bush to draw blood, threw the bloodied shuttle into the well, and jumped in after it.

When she came to, she found herself in the same meadow her stepsister had awakened in. She walked until she came to the loaves of bread crying to be removed from the baker's oven. "What!" cried the lazy girl. "And soil my dress with flour!" Then she went on until she came to the apples crying to be shaken free. "What! And be hit on the head with a shower of apples!" she said. And on she went until she reached the cottage.

As she had done with the stepdaughter, Mother Hulda came forth from the cottage to invite the sister to keep house for her. The lazy sister accepted, knowing that riches lay in store for her. Then she set out to do the chores as best she could. She shook the bed until a feather or two flew. She managed to be polite to Mother Hulda. But she soon grew tired and told Mother Hulda to send her home.

Mother Hulda handed the girl her shuttle and led her to the great door. But instead of sending her to earth in a shower of gold, Mother Hulda sent her to earth in a shower of pitch. As the girl crossed the yard to her home, the rooster cried:

> "Cock-a-doodle doo!
> Your dirty girl's come back to you."

And the pitch clung to the lazy girl for the rest of her life.

The Star Dippe[r]

Now, a girl lived with her mother in a cottage at the edge of a wood. One summer night, the mother did not feel well. "I am so thirsty," she said. "I wish I had a drink of cold water."

The little girl was very kind and thoughtful. "I will get you a drink, Mother," she said, slipping on her dress and shoes. She took an old tin dipper and ran out to the well in the yard. She pulled up the bucket, but not a drop of water was in it.

"What shall I do?" said the little girl. "It is so warm, and Mother is so weak and thirsty. I will go to the spring. Surely there will be water in the spring."

The spring was way off in the woods, and it was a very dark night, but the little girl tried not to be afraid as she ran down the path to the woods. It was darker still in the woods, and she soon lost the path. Sharp stones cut through her shoes. Big stones tripped her.

"Oh, where is that spring?" cried the little girl. "Mother is so very thirsty, and I simply cannot turn back."

At last she heard a trickling sound, and she knew she had come to the spring. She knelt down and filled the old tin dipper. Then she started home.

Soon she met a little dog. He was panting, and his pink tongue was hanging from his mouth. "Poor little dog, you must be thirsty. The brooks are all dry. I will give you a drink of this cold water. I have filled the dipper for my mother, but there is enough for you, too." She poured some water into her cupped hand, and the dog lapped it up eagerly.

The little girl continued on her way. Soon she noticed that it had grown lighter. The light seemed to come from her hand. She looked down and saw that the old tin dipper had turned to silver. It was bright and shone like the moon. She could walk much faster with the help of the light from the dipper.

After a while, the little girl met an old man. "Little girl," he asked, "can you tell me where I can get a drink of cold water? The brooks are all dry."

"I will give you a drink," said the little girl. And she gave him some water.

The old man thanked her and went on his way. But as soon as he was gone, she noticed that it had grown even lighter than before. She looked down and saw that the silver dipper had turned to gold. It shone like the sun. And since she could see even better than before, it was not long before she reached home.

"I have brought you a drink of cold spring water," said the little girl.

"Thank you, my good little girl," said the mother. "How much better I feel!"

Then the little girl and her mother noticed bright lights flashing on the walls of the house. They looked down and saw that the dipper had changed to sparkling diamonds.

Out of the window went the diamonds, high up into the sky. The little girl and her mother stood in the doorway, watching as they turned to seven bright, twinkling stars—a dipper in the sky.

It was many, many years ago that the kind little girl and her mother lived. But if you look into the sky some bright, starry night, you will still see the dipper.

The Babes in the Wood

Once there lived a noble lord and lady who had two children whom they loved dearly. Willie, the eldest, was five and was a fine little fellow. Jenny, a year younger, was fair-haired and pretty and the darling of the household. Their's was a happy household, until one sad day when the lord and lady took ill.

When they knew they were about to die, they sent for their brother. They begged him to love and care for their two babes. "They will be no burden as far as money goes," said the lord, "for to Willie I have left three hundred pieces of gold a year, and to Jenny five hundred."

As soon as the parents were dead, the two babes went to live with their uncle. The uncle tried to be as kind to them as it was in his nature to be. But his nature, alas, was wicked and dishonest. He wanted the children's gold, and it was not long before he had plotted a way to get rid of them and get their money.

The uncle paid two ruffians two bags of gold each to take the babes deep into the woods and kill them. He told the babes that he was sending them away to London, in the charge of two honest men, there to be brought up properly.

The next morning, the two trusting babes rode off with the ruffians. After many hours of riding, they entered a thick, dark wood.

"Is this the way to London?" Willie asked boldly. "I do not like this dark, wild wood."

Little Jenny had gone without her usual midday nap, and she was sleepy. So she kissed the ruffian who carried her on his horse and then, laying her cheek against him, fell fast asleep. The tender gesture softened this ruffian's heart toward the children. He determined to save them.

"Comrade," he said, "let us not hurt these children. They never harmed us. And who is ever to know that we did not complete this foul task?"

But his partner had a hard heart. "We have been well paid," he answered roughly. "I, for one, intend to earn my wage."

The kind-hearted ruffian continued to plead on behalf of the babes. Soon the men were arguing, and soon after they came to blows. The kind-hearted ruffian drove off the hard-hearted one. Then he, too, rode off, promising to return to the babes with cakes and fruit.

Night fell, and no one came for Willie and Jenny. Tired and hungry and lost, the babes began to cry. The animals heard the children and looked on sadly. A little brown bird, perched high on a tree limb, looked down on them and said to her mate, "Our children are safe in their warm nest, but these dear babes will die of cold and hunger before the morning." Then she and her mate began to trill the sweetest lullaby ever sung.

Comforted, the two lost babes lay down side by side, with their arms around each other. The tears dried on their cheeks, and they were soon sound asleep.

That night, the babes died peacefully in each other's arms. The birds and the beasts gathered leaves from the bushes and trees and tenderly covered the poor babes. Willie and Jenny suffered no more.

The Real Princess

Once a prince lived in a castle with his aging parents, the king and queen. No sooner had the prince come of age than the king and queen urged him to go out and find himself a young lady to marry. You see, they were eager to have royal grandsons and grand-daughters. Not just any young lady would do, however. Only a real princess could become the prince's wife.

The prince traveled throughout the world in search of a real princess. But times were hard. While once there had been thousands of princesses, now there was a shortage in the land. And with the few princesses remaining, the prince always found something the matter.

One night, a terrible storm blew up. It thundered. It lightninged. It rained in frightful quantities. In the midst of this storm, there came a knocking at the castle door. The old king went to see who could be out on such a night.

At the door, dripping wet, stood a princess. Water streamed from her straggly hair, down her dress, and into her shoes. She was a sight! But she claimed nevertheless to be a real prin-cess. And she wished to be granted shelter for the night.

"A real princess, eh?" said the queen, casting a doubtful eye on the visitor. "We'll see about that!" And without another word, she hurried off to the spare bedroom. Removing all the bedding, she carefully placed a single tiny dried pea

in the center of the mattress. Over the pea, she placed twenty more mattresses. And over the mattresses, she placed twenty feather quilts. Then she led the princess, who by now had received a warm bath and dry bedclothes, to the spare bedroom.

In the morning, the princess came down to join the royal family at breakfast.

"Did you sleep well, my dear?" they all asked.

"Sleep!" she groaned. "I hardly slept a wink the whole night." Indeed, there were great dark circles beneath her eyes.

"As a matter of fact," the princess continued, "I have never spent a more dreadful night. There was some sort of lump in my bed. It was so hard that I am black and blue all over."

Everyone was enormously pleased (except for the princess, of course), for who but a real princess could have felt a tiny pea through twenty mattresses and twenty feather quilts? Only a real princess could have such delicate feelings.

And so it came to pass that the royal family's dearest wish was fulfilled at last. The prince and the real princess (who was now delighted, since the prince was so handsome) were married with great pomp and splendor.

As for the pea that had brought the prince and the princess together, it was set on a velvet cushion and carefully placed in a special glass case kept in a room at the top of the castle. If you knew just where to look, you could probably find it there today.

Hansel and Gretel

O n the outskirts of a vast forest, there lived a brother and sister named Hansel and Gretel. Their father was a poor woodcutter, and the family was often hungry.

Their stepmother grew tired of this hard life, and one night she told the woodcutter, "Four mouths are too many to feed. Tomorrow we must take the children deep into the forest and leave them."

"No, wife," the woodcutter said. "If we were all to starve, I could not do that."

"Well, if you cannot, I will," said the stepmother.

Hansel heard his mother's wicked plan as he lay in bed. When the old people were asleep, he got up, slipped on his coat, opened the back door, and stole out. The moon shone brightly, and the white pebbles in front of the house glittered like silver. Hansel filled his pocket with many stones. Then he went back to bed.

At daybreak, the woman came to wake the children. "Get up. We are going to the forest to gather wood."

After packing some bread for lunch, they set out together into the forest. Hansel brought up the rear and, every few paces, dropped a pebble. When they reached the middle of the forest, the stepmother said, "Now, children, go and find some kindling wood."

Hansel and Gretel collected wood until, tired from their efforts, they fell asleep. When they awoke, it was pitch dark and they were all alone. Gretel began to cry. "Don't cry," said Hansel. "The moon will soon come up."

When the moon had risen, he took his sister by the hand. Together they followed the pebbles, which led them back to their father's house by daybreak.

Their father was overjoyed to see them, but their stepmother was not. "Lazy things," she snapped. "Where is my kindling wood?" And she led them right back into the woods and left them there. This time, Hansel had left behind a trail of bread crumbs instead of pebbles. But the birds had eaten every crumb.

Now the children were truly lost. They wandered the woods until they came to a lovely cottage made of bread. The window panes were made of thin sugar. The roof was made of cake.

Hansel and Gretel began to nibble at the house, for they were very hungry. A shrill voice called out from inside:

"Nibble, nibble, little mouse,
Who is nibbling at my house?"

Then an old woman leaning on a stick peeped out the door. "Come inside," she said, "and share my supper instead."

The children gladly joined her, for they did not know that she was really a witch who captured children, fattened them up, and ate them. As soon as the children were inside, the old woman locked Hansel in a cage.

Each day for a week, the witch tested Hansel's plumpness by feeling one of his fingers. Each day Hansel fooled her. Instead of a finger, he held out a small chicken bone for her to feel. Soon the witch grew tired. Since Hansel wasn't getting any plumper, she would have to eat both children.

The witch opened the oven door and said to Gretel, "See if it is hot enough for bread, dear."

Gretel pretended not to understand. "Show me how to tell," said Gretel.

The witch opened the door still wider, and Gretel pushed her inside and slammed the door shut. The witch burned to a cinder. Then Gretel unlocked Hansel's cage, and the children ran off.

Looking for a path home, the children met their father, who had been searching for them for days. While they were gone, their stepmother had mysteriously died, he told them. Thus all their troubles were ended, and they would live happily ever afterward.

The Country Mouse and the City Mouse

A city mouse paid his country cousin a visit. When the country mouse had finished giving his cousin a tour of the fields and the big red barn, they sat down to a dinner of barley and grain. The country mouse ate heartily, but the city mouse only nibbled.

"Don't you like barley and grain?" asked the country mouse.

"Not very much, dear cousin," answered the city mouse. "I don't want to seem impolite, but I wish you could taste the fine things I eat every day. You must come to the city and visit."

So the country mouse went to the city to visit. "You must be hungry after your trip from the country," said the city mouse. "We will go to the pantry and have a taste of real food."

The city mouse led the way through a hole into the kitchen pantry. The country mouse had never seen so many jars and bags and boxes. "Oh, what luck!" cried the city mouse. "The bread box is open."

They crept inside, and the country mouse saw something big and round and brown. "This," said the proud city mouse, "is chocolate cake. Taste it, and see how you like it."

The country mouse nibbled at the cake. How sweet it was! "How lucky you are, dear cousin," the country mouse was saying, when the door opened, and a big, rosy-cheeked woman walked into the pantry.

"Run for the hole!" whispered the city mouse. And the two mice scampered back into the hole.

When they were safe inside, the city mouse said, "Don't look so frightened, cousin. That was only the cook. She may not like us, but she cannot catch us. We will go back as soon as she's gone."

After a while, the city mouse looked out and saw that the coast was clear. Back to the pantry went the two mice.

This time the city mouse showed his cousin a box. "There is something good

inside," he said, and they began to gnaw a hole in one corner. Then the country mouse tasted something even more delicious than chocolate cake. The city mouse told him that the box was filled with raisins.

Suddenly, the mice heard a scratching at the door. "Run for cover!" whispered the city mouse.

When they were safely back in the hole, the city mouse said, "Don't tremble so, dear cousin. That was only the cat. She will soon go away."

The country mouse could not stop trembling. "I would rather not go back to the pantry," he said.

"All right," said the city mouse. "The nicest thing for mice is in the cellar."

They scampered down the stairs to the cellar cupboard. The country mouse thought it was the most wonderful place he had ever seen. On the floor were barrels of apples. From the ceiling hung strings of sausages. The two mice ran about, nibbling here and nibbling there.

The country mouse saw something of a deep yellow color. It smelled very good. He took a nibble. It had a most delicious taste. "That is cheese," his city cousin said. "There is nothing better."

The country mouse saw another piece of cheese. It was fastened to a queer little square stand. He was just about to take a big bite when the city mouse called out, "Stop! Don't eat that. It is in a trap."

"What is a trap?" asked the country mouse.

"Something hard," said the city mouse, "that comes down on your neck. With it, you could never eat again."

"Oh," said the country mouse, trembling. "I think I must be going home right away. You have been kind to give me all these things to eat, but I would rather eat my barley and grain in safety."

So the country mouse went home to the country. He ate barley and grain in peace and comfort for the rest of his days.

The Traveling Musicians of Bremen

An old donkey, upon realizing that his master was planning to sell him for his hide, ran away on the road to Bremen. He had made up his mind to become a street musician. Soon he came upon an old hunting hound lying exhausted in the gutter.

"What ails you, Old Boy?" he asked the dog.

"Oh!" moaned the dog. "My master beats me when I fail to catch rabbits. Every day he beats me harder, and every day the rabbits run faster. Soon I'll be put to death, I'm sure."

"Why not come with me?" said the donkey. "I'm off to Bremen to become a street musician."

The dog agreed to this, and together they set off. Soon they met up with a dejected old cat.

"What seems to be the problem, Gray Whiskers?" asked the donkey.

"I'm too old to catch mice, and my mistress plans to drown me," said the cat.

"Then come with us to Bremen. You would make an excellent singer."

The cat joined the donkey and the dog, and the three continued on their way. Shortly, they came upon a rooster crowing with all his might.

"Whatever's the matter, Chanticleer?" asked the donkey. "Why are you crowing so?"

"My master plans to eat me in a stew, for I promised him good weather and it rained."

"Nonsense," said the donkey. "Come along with us. You've a splendid voice which would give tone to our band."

The rooster agreed, and they proceeded on their way. By evening they had reached a great forest. The rooster flew into a tree to look about and spied a light.

Upon reaching the house from which the light came, the donkey looked in the window. He saw a well-laden table with several thieves seated round it. If only they could get at that food!

The musicians worked out a plan. The donkey stood with his forelegs on the windowsill. The dog climbed on the donkey's back. The cat climbed on top of the dog's head, and the rooster perched on the head of the cat. Then they began to make music. The donkey brayed, the dog barked, the cat yowled, the rooster crowed, and all four crashed through the window.

The thieves, thinking they were being attacked by a demon, ran from the house, whereupon the four musicians sat down and ate their fill. Then each went to sleep in the place of his choice.

Meanwhile, the thieves decided they should not have been so easily frightened. One of them went back to investigate.

The thief entered the dark house. Mistaking the cat's glowing eyes for coals, he tried to strike a match from them. The cat sprang at his face, spitting and scratching. The startled thief ran out the door and tripped over the dog, who bit him in the leg. As he ran across the yard, the donkey gave him a sound kick, while the rooster on the roof crowed, "Cock-a-doodle-do!"

Terrified, the thief returned to his comrades. "There's a witch in there," he said, "who scratched me with a knife, and a black monster in the yard who hit me with a club. And upon the roof sits a judge, who cried, 'Bring the rogue here!'"

With this, the thieves fled, never to return. That perfectly suited the four musicians, who lived happily in the house the rest of their lives.

The Shoema[...]

That's the last of the leather," said the good shoemaker to his wife. "And that's the last pair of shoes I can cut. I'll sew them in the morning."

That night they went to bed worried. They had little to live on. Business had not been good and, with no more leather and no money to buy any, it could only get worse.

The next morning, the good shoemaker was amazed to find on his workbench not the leather pieces but a pair of shoes, finished and sewn with fine neat stitches. "This must be magic!" he declared to his wife. "It would take me a week to make such shoes."

That day, a lady came into the store and paid him handsomely for the shoes. The shoemaker was now able to buy enough leather for two new pairs.

In the evening, he cut out two pairs of shoes and laid the pieces on the bench before going to bed. When he came downstairs in the morning, he found two pairs of finished shoes, as finely and neatly stitched as the first pair.

That day, customers bought the shoes. With the money he got for them, the shoemaker was able to buy leather for four more pairs. In the evening, he cut out the pieces and laid them on the bench. In the morning, four pairs of finished shoes lay in their place.

And so it went. Each night he left out a number of pairs of shoes ready to be stitched, and every morning he found them finished and ready to be sold.

One day, the shoemaker's wife said, "Let us stay up tonight and see who it is who helps us."

"Better not," said the shoemaker, "for this is magic, and it is best not to be curious about matters of magic."

"But if we see these 'magicians,' we

d the Elves

might find some way to repay them," said the good wife.

The shoemaker agreed, and that night, instead of going to bed, they lit a candle and peeped out from between the folds of the curtains.

After the clock had struck midnight, two little naked men came through the window. Without a word, they hopped onto the bench and set to work stitching the leather pieces. How the tiny fingers flew! Before long, all the leather had been made into shoes. Then the two little men joined hands and pranced and skipped about. As the clock struck two, they skipped out the window.

"Poor little men," said the shoemaker's wife, when she was sure they had gone. "They looked so bare and cold. I think I will make them each a little suit."

"What a fine idea!" said the shoemaker. "And I will make them each shoes."

"And instead of setting out work for them tonight, we shall set out our presents," said the wife.

The next day, the good wife sewed two little coats of fine green cloth and two little waistcoats of yellow, two little pairs of trousers of blue and two little caps of red. The shoemaker made two tiny pairs of shoes of soft red leather.

After supper, they laid out the tiny outfits and two tiny servings of supper. Then they went to bed.

As the clock struck twelve, the two little men pranced through the window and skipped over to the bench. When they saw the two little suits of clothes, they chuckled with delight and put them on immediately. Then they sat down and ate. When they had finished, they went prancing and skipping out the window.

The shoemaker and his wife never saw the elves again. But the elves must have left them luck, for the good couple never again wanted for anything.

The Sugar-Plum Tree

ave you ever heard of the Sugar-Plum Tree?
　'Tis a marvel of great renown!
It blooms on the shore of the Lollipop Sea
　In the garden of Shut-Eye Town.
The fruit that it bears is so wondrously sweet
　(And those who have tasted it say)
That the good little children have only to eat
　Of that fruit to be happy next day.
When you've got to the tree, you would have a hard time
　To capture the fruit which I sing;
The tree is so tall that no person could climb
　To the boughs where the sugar-plums swing!
But up in that tree sits a chocolate cat,
　And a gingerbread dog prowls below—
And this is the way you contrive to get at
　Those sugar-plums tempting you so:

You say but a word to that gingerbread dog
　And he barks with such terrible zest
That the chocolate cat is at once all agog,
　As her swelling proportions attest.
And the chocolate cat goes cavorting around
　From this leafy limb unto that,
And the sugar-plums tumble, of course, to the ground—
　Hurrah for that chocolate cat!
There are marshmallows, gumdrops, and peppermint
　　canes,
　With stripings of scarlet and gold,
And you carry away of the treasure that rains
　As much as your apron can hold!
So come, little child, cuddle closer to me
　In your dainty white nightcap and gown,
And I'll rock you away to that Sugar-Plum Tree
　In the garden of Shut-Eye Town.

—Eugene Field

The Owl
and the Pussycat

The Owl and the Pussycat went to sea
    In a beautiful pea-green boat:
They took some honey and plenty of money
    Wrapped up in a five-pound note.
The Owl looked up to the stars above,
    And sang to a small guitar,
"O lovely Pussy, O Pussy, my love,
    What a beautiful Pussy you are,
        You are,
        You are!
    What a beautiful Pussy you are!"

Pussy said to the Owl, "You elegant fowl,
    How charmingly sweet you sing!
Oh, let us be married; too long we have tarried;
    But what shall we do for a ring?"
They sailed away for a year and a day,
    To a land where the bong tree grows;

And there in a wood a Piggy-wig stood,
   With a ring at the end of his nose,
     His nose,
     His nose,
   With a ring at the end of his nose.

"Dear Pig, are you willing to sell for one shilling
   Your ring?" Said the Piggy, "I will."
So they took it away and were married next day
   By the Turkey who lives on the hill.
They dined on mince and slices of quince,
   Which they ate with a runcible spoon;
And hand in hand, on the edge of the sand,
   They danced by the light of the moon,
     The moon,
     The moon,
They danced by the light of the moon.

              — Edward Lear

Escape at Bedtime

he lights from the parlor and kitchen shone out
   Through the blinds and the windows and bars;
And high overhead and all moving about,
   There were thousands of millions of stars.
There ne'er were such thousands of leaves on a tree,
   Nor of people in church or the park,
As the crowds of the stars that looked down upon me,
   And that glittered and winked in the dark.
The Dog, and the Plough, and the Hunter, and all,
   And the Star of the Sailor, and Mars,
These shone in the sky, and the pail by the wall
   Would be half full of water and stars.
They saw me at last, and they chased me with cries,
   And they soon had me packed into bed;
But the glory kept shining and bright in my eyes,
   And the stars going round in my head.

—Robert Louis Stevenson

One of the world's foremost illustrators of children's books, Tasha Tudor has always had a special feeling for the world of folk and fairy tales. This has never been more apparent than it is in her *Bedtime Book*.

The daughter of Rosamond Tudor, who was a portrait painter, and W. Starling Burgess, who designed yachts, Miss Tudor studied at the Museum of Fine Arts in Boston. Though she was born in that city, she grew up on a farm in Connecticut, and she has never lost her enthusiasm for country life, especially for New England. She now lives in Vermont in a house built by her son, where she is surrounded by her corgis, her family, and friends.